JUN 2 6 2020

W9-ANU-973

dabble lab

SHOOT EPIC SHORT DOCUMENTARIES

4D An Augmented Reading Experience

by Thomas Kingsley Troupe

Consultant:

Diana L. Rendina, MLIS
Media Specialist, Speaker, Writer
Tampa, FL

CAPSTONE PRESS
a capstone imprint

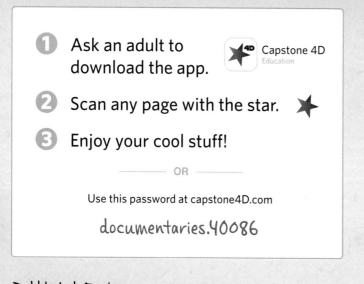

1. Ask an adult to download the app.

Capstone 4D
Education

2. Scan any page with the star.

3. Enjoy your cool stuff!

— OR —

Use this password at capstone4D.com

documentaries.40086

Dabble Lab Books are published by Capstone Press
1710 Roe Crest Drive
North Mankato, Minnesota 56003
www.mycapstone.com

Library of Congress Cataloging-in-Publication Data
Library of Congress Cataloging-in-Publication Data is available on the Library of Congress website.
Names: Troupe, Thomas Kingsley, author.
ISBN 978-1-5435-4008-6 (hardcover)
ISBN 978-1-5435-4016-1 (eBook PDF)

Editorial Credits

Shelly Lyons, editor; Sarah Bennett, designer; Morgan Walters, media researcher; Katy LaVigne, production specialist

Photo Credits

All photos by Capstone Studio, Karon Dubke, except: iStockphoto: FatCamera, 32; Shutterstock: Arvind Balaraman, 11, Astarina, design element, Becris, design element, bonandbon, 8, Can Yesil, design element, Darcraft, design element, David Porras, bottom 9, Grisha Bruev, Cover, handini_atmodiwiryo, (books) 26 Havoc, bottom 39, hxdbzxy, top 22, Jason Korbol, top 39, Kzenon, 19, Lightspring, background 45, Lisa F. Young, 13, Luigi Bertello, 15, MIKHAIL GRACHIKOV, cover, Monkey Business Images, top 9, Natasha Pankina, design element, Naumenko Aleksandr, spread 22-23, pixelheadphoto digitalskillet, 18, PK Studio, 12, Ramona Kaulitzki, 16, Seth Gallmeyer, design element, Shorena Tedliashvili, design element, silm, design element, vector illustration, design element, Vissay, bottom 45, www.hollandfoto.net, 21, yanin kongurai, 11

All internet sites, apps, and software programs appearing in back matter were available and accurate when this book was sent to press.

Printed and bound in China.
1671

CONTENTS

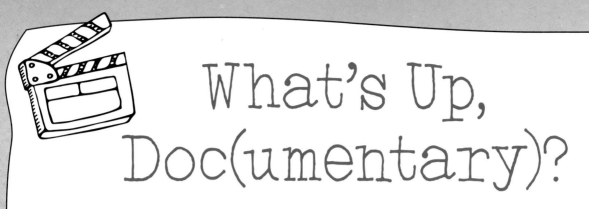

What's Up, Doc(umentary)?

A local hero tells the story of how he saved a family from a car wreck. A narrator gives us a behind-the-scenes look at a famous pizza shop. Are these videos part of the evening news? No, they're short documentaries! Short documentaries are nonfiction videos about real people, events, and places. They're designed to educate viewers. A documentary filmmaker talks with people and visits locations to bring these interesting stories to life.

Documentary Success Guide

Be Patient Filmmaking is something that takes practice. You won't make a perfect movie the first time, the second time, or ever. As difficult as it can sound, practice makes *better*, never perfect.

Keep It Interesting One of the best things about making a documentary is finding a subject that really interests you. If you are passionate about something, that feeling will show through your work.

Capture Everything When making a documentary, there is no such thing as wasted footage. Ask lots of questions and capture everything you can. Though you might not want to use everything you shoot, it's good to have a lot of options to choose from.

What You'll Need:

☆ an idea
☆ a script
☆ a storyboard
☆ a subject
☆ a video camera, tablet, or phone camera
☆ a microphone
☆ a location
☆ lights
☆ editing software

Filming a short documentary video doesn't need to be expensive. You can find everything you need around the house. Use what you have and capture your vision without breaking the bank.

It's All About the Camera

Digital Cameras

One of your most important filmmaking tools will be your camera. Find a digital camera that is simple to use and able to record long shots of video. Make sure there is plenty of room on the camera's memory card.

Smartphones & Tablets

If you can use a smartphone or a tablet as your camera, you're in luck. Not only are they small and easy to use, many of them have apps for video-editing built in. If not, you can always add one. Be sure to have an adult help you download the app you need. Also, make sure there's enough memory available for all of your video footage.

Ideas

A great documentary starts with a good idea. Pick a topic that you and others are interested in. Your neighborhood alone is filled with interesting people and places.

Shoot a video about the local firehouse and interview the firefighters. Visit a pet shelter and learn about how they help animals find new homes. There are stories everywhere! They are just waiting to be told and shared with the world.

PRO TIP

One of the best ways to drum up inspiration is to watch some of the other (kid-friendly) documentaries out there. Ask an adult to help you find some good examples.

Can I be in your documentary?

Treatment and Research

Treatment

One of the first things to do when starting a documentary is to create a treatment. A treatment is a game plan for your video. In a treatment, you write down what you want to capture during filming.

Let's say you're doing a documentary about your local ice-cream shop. Plans can change, but having a treatment is a way to get your good idea on paper. It's a great starting point. Ask yourself a few simple questions to help guide your treatment:

TREATMENT

What is the goal of the documentary?

— The goal is to learn about how a small ice-cream shop operates, what makes it special, and how someone can open his/her own shop.

How will you accomplish this?

— I'll achieve my goal by interviewing the ice-cream shop owners/workers and doing research on the company.

Where will this be filmed?

— I'll shoot video in the ice-cream shop (with permission).

What's the goal of my documentary?

Is this a reliable source of information?

Research

A documentary should be as factually accurate as possible. It's best to research your topic. Find as much information as you can in books, on the internet, or even by talking to subject matter experts. Don't be afraid to ask a librarian for help.

Write down any information that might be useful or interesting for your audience. Giving your viewers a lot of background facts will make your film stronger. Not sure which ones to include? Think about the facts that made you say, "Whoa! I never knew that!" Chances are, if YOU found it interesting, your viewers will too.

PRO TIP

It's important to use good sources. Make sure the "experts" you interview know what they're talking about. Use facts only from reliable internet sites. News organizations, museums, and colleges are good sites to use as sources. A librarian can help you determine if a site is reliable or not.

Write a Script

Now that you've got a plan in place and have done some research, it's time to write a script. Using your treatment as a guide, build an outline. Somewhere in the beginning of the script, you should explain the goal of your documentary. Then plan where you'll put your facts and interviews.

Example:

Since 2001, Scoop O' Fun has been operating in my hometown. Now, 18 years later, people are still going crazy for the ice cream they sell. In this film, we'll learn how the company started and why people are still excited about their ice cream.

When writing a script, don't worry about making it look like a REAL Hollywood script. Describe the scene you want to shoot, who or what is there, and what's happening. Most of all, the script serves as a plan for what you hope to capture in the scene. It also helps you stay organized. There's nothing worse than finishing up and realizing you forgot to film an important shot.

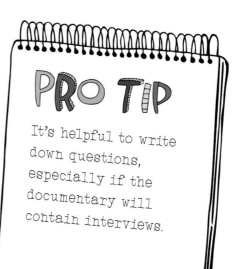

PRO TIP

It's helpful to write down questions, especially if the documentary will contain interviews.

SCRIPT

		Video	Audio
Shot 1		Full shot of the shop's storefront. People enter the building.	Small town ice-cream shops have been around for many years. They're a popular place for summer treats. But how do they operate? What makes this ice-cream shop so special?
Shot 2		Close-up of ice-cream buckets in the display. A worker scoops some ice cream and places the scoop on a cone.	We hear background noise here—people chatting, cash register ringing, etc.
Shot 3		Customer grabs the cone—a big smile on her face. The worker and customer exchange dialogue.	Worker: "Enjoy your cone." Customer: "Thanks."

15

Draw a Storyboard

Just as a script helps you organize what's going to happen and what might be said, a storyboard helps you decide how your video will look. The storyboard helps you plan where to put the camera for each shot. In a storyboard, each scene is one panel, much like the panels in a comic strip.

scene #1
Full shot of the shop's storefront. People enter the building.
Intro narration: " ... "

scene #2
Close-up of ice-cream buckets in the display. A worker scoops some ice cream and places the scoop on a cone.

scene #3
Customer grabs the cone—a big smile on her face.
The worker and customer exchange dialogue.

scene #4
Cut to wide-angle shot of the store; happy customers.

scene #5

scene #6

Don't worry about making your storyboard a work of art. If you're filming the outside of a building, sketch it! You can draw each and every shot, or you can roughly sketch what the scene might look like. The storyboard will be a checklist of the shots you'll need to finish your documentary.

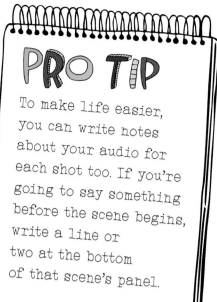

PRO TIP

To make life easier, you can write notes about your audio for each shot too. If you're going to say something before the scene begins, write a line or two at the bottom of that scene's panel.

scene #7

Close-up of owner meeting interviewer.

scene #8

Cut to owner and interviewer eating ice cream at a table.

scene #9

Interview begins.

Use prepared interview questions here.

scene #10

Cut to close-up of the vanilla ice-cream recipe.

scene #11

scene #12

Seeking Subjects

Casting ☆ Subjects ☆ Actors

Now it's time find people to be in your documentary. Make a list of the individuals you'd like to interview. Realize that some of them may not be available or interested, or they may live too far away.

Can you interview someone from the ice-cream shop? Are frequent customers available to be in your movie? Finding a good variety of people to interview will make your documentary stronger.

happy customers ☺

ice-cream
shop owner

19

Set Up Interviews

Using your list of potential subjects/interviewees, try to contact them to see if they would be willing to participate. Explain what the intent of your documentary is and when you'd like to talk with them. With an adult's help, schedule a good time and place to meet for an interview.

INTERVIEW QUESTIONS

1. How long has your ice-cream shop been in business?

2. Why do you think customers keep coming back?

3. What makes this shop special?

4. What advice would you have for someone who wants to open an ice-cream shop?

PRO TIP

If possible, send your interviewees a list of questions ahead of time. They'll be happy to have more time to think of thoughtful answers. Plus, happy interviewees will be more likely to help you out when needed.

In some cases, you'll want to meet with your interviewees at their homes or places of business. Again, it's best to have an adult with you to make sure you and your equipment are safe.

Pick a Location

Try to find a place that's visually interesting. A blank, empty room isn't exciting to look at.

Are you interviewing an author? Film her in front of a large shelf of books or in a library. Meeting with a teacher at school? Shoot the video in the classroom. Anything you can do to connect your subject to your audience will be helpful and engaging. If you can film inside the ice-cream shop, do it. But make sure you get permission to do so, and ask an adult to go with you.

PRO TIP

Avoid white, bland backgrounds and spaces for your interviews. While the conversation should be interesting enough, it's best to have fun settings for your viewers to look at.

Light Up the Set

Your viewers should be able to see what you're filming. Do your best to get plenty of light on your subjects and backgrounds without making it TOO bright. Overhead light fixtures and lamps work well, but be careful with fluorescent lights. They can make people look washed out and sometimes green.

poor lighting ☹

Natural light can be a nice touch in documentaries, but the light quality will change throughout the day. That can be problematic for longer shoots. If you're doing a quick one- or two-hour scene, go for it!

PRO TIP

Take some test footage to see if you like how the light looks. If it seems too dim or too bright, make adjustments.

better lighting

Unless you're planning to film while walking, it's best to put your camera on a tripod. A tripod will keep the camera in place so the video isn't shaky. You can find inexpensive tripods for both cameras and phones/tablets. If you don't have a tripod, make a stack of books and set the camera on top.

← phone tripod

Decide on a good place to set up. You should be able to see the subject and background.
If you do need to go "handheld" (without a tripod), be sure your fingers don't get in the way of the lens.

PRO TIP

Don't feel that you have to keep the camera in the same spot for a whole scene. Move the camera to the side or get some close-ups. Be creative! Getting a few different angles will help keep things interesting for the viewer.

Shoot the Video!

Ready to finally start filming? Perfect! With the lights, camera, and talent in position, you can begin recording. If you're interviewing people for your documentary, introduce them or have them introduce themselves. Then you can begin asking questions that support the goal of your documentary.

Follow your script and storyboard. They'll help you stay on track and reach your goals for the documentary.

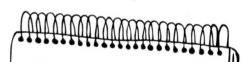

PRO TIP

Friends can help! Ask a friend to conduct the interview. Another friend can run the camera while you act as the director. The director decides on camera angles and where to position subjects.

Documentary filmmaking is much different from making other types of movies. Don't feel as if you need to stop recording after each question. Let the shot continue so you're not stopping and starting over and over.

PRO TIP

If you have two cameras, you can keep one on the subject and another on the interviewer. Doubling the footage will give you TONS of options when it's time to edit.

Keep the camera rolling and moving. Movement and different angles will give your audience a mix of things to watch, and it will keep them interested. When you cut, consider moving the camera to capture your subject another way.

Cutaways

Giving the audience a break from seeing a bunch of talking heads is important. People tend to have short attention spans. Between interviews or topics, it's sometimes good to cut away to a shot of something else. Consider cutting away to a scenic location, an interesting object in the room, or even something you see out the window.

Cutaways are also great places to add narration between scenes. If you've got an interesting fact to share with your audience, an image of something different might be the best place for it.

Shot 12 Cutaway: close-up of kittens in a holding space for cats

Audio: Interview is taking place.

Meow!

Shot Options

To keep your video interesting, you need some variety! Adjust the camera, film different things in the room, or film from different angles. Try these:

Pan and Tilt Shots—moving the camera from left to right (pan) or moving the camera up or down (tilt)

 pan shot (left to right)

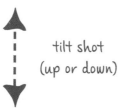 tilt shot (up or down)

PRO TIP

Capture as much as possible when shooting. Don't worry about having too much footage. You can decide what to keep and what to cut later. Having more than you need is better than needing more than you have!

Exterior Shot—showing the location where the interview or filming is taking place; if you're filming inside a pet shelter, for example, film a bit of the outside of the building; exterior shots help your audience get a clear sense of the location

Close-Up—getting up close and personal to the person, object, or place you're filming

Zoom—using the built-in zoom feature to move closer to (zoom in) or farther away from (zoom out) the object you're filming; this is sometimes a sliding bar or a button on a digital camera

wide-angle
(pull camera back)

Wide-Angle—pulling the camera back so more of the scene can be seen

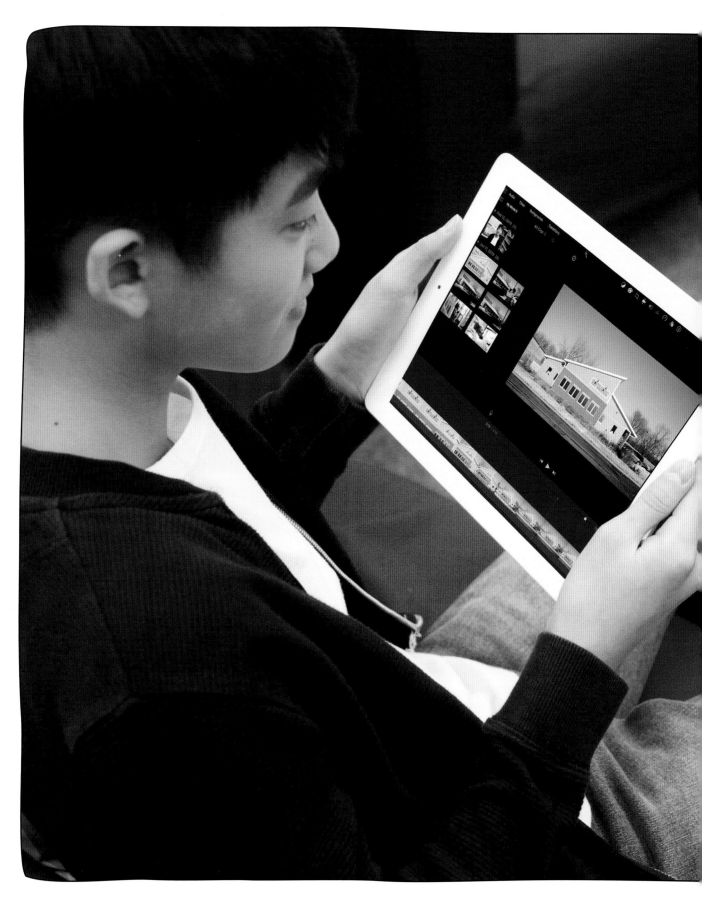

Cut It Up

Rough Cut

Once you've shot everything in your script and storyboard, it's time to edit your masterpiece. Editing is like putting together a puzzle with many pieces. You take the video clips you've shot and put them together in a way that makes sense.

First, pull all of your video clips into the editing app/software. (Check page 48 for suggested editing programs.) Using your script as your guide, put the clips in the correct order. Once you've got all the clips you want to use "roughed" in, click play to watch your rough cut.

PRO TIP

When watching the rough cut of your video, be on the lookout for parts that do and don't work. Take notes, so it will be easier to figure out where to make edits.

Cutting

Now comes the tough part. It's time to get rid of the things that didn't work so well. You don't want your documentary to be too long. The key is to keep people interested. Don't bore your viewers!

Is there a long pause between questions? Cut out the extra space. Is there a clip that just doesn't seem very interesting? Say goodbye! If you don't like something in your documentary, don't be afraid to get rid of it.

☒ Cut the time between questions in this clip.

Oops! Delete this clip.

Cute! Use this clip for a cutaway.

PRO TIP

Add cutaway shots or extra footage between interview questions or scenes. They will help break things up a bit and will give your viewers a variety of things to look at.

Narration ☆ Music

Watch your freshly edited documentary. Does it seem like something is missing? It might need a couple of things. Adding some narration to the documentary will give it a personal touch. Talk about your movie's topic and what you hope to accomplish with the video. Explain why you're interviewing the people in the documentary. It's YOUR documentary, put your voice on it!

Ever watch a movie without music? It can feel flat and lifeless. Documentaries can benefit from music too. Adding even a little music to your video will spruce it up a lot.

PRO TIP

Be sure to add only music that you have permission to use. You could get in trouble for using "popular" music and may be asked to remove it from your documentary!

Almost There!

When your film is edited, it's time for some finishing touches. During the course of filming, did you think of a title? Add the title to your documentary so people know what to call it. While most editing apps have built-in title generators, you could design one on your own and film it.

Chances are, you didn't work on the documentary all by yourself. Be sure to add the names of your crew to the credits. Thank anyone you interviewed or who helped you find information. As with the title, you can get creative with how your credits display.

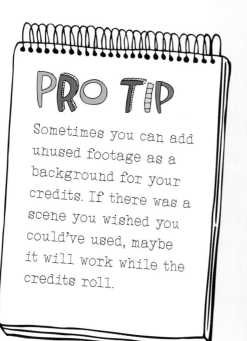

PRO TIP

Sometimes you can add unused footage as a background for your credits. If there was a scene you wished you could've used, maybe it will work while the credits roll.

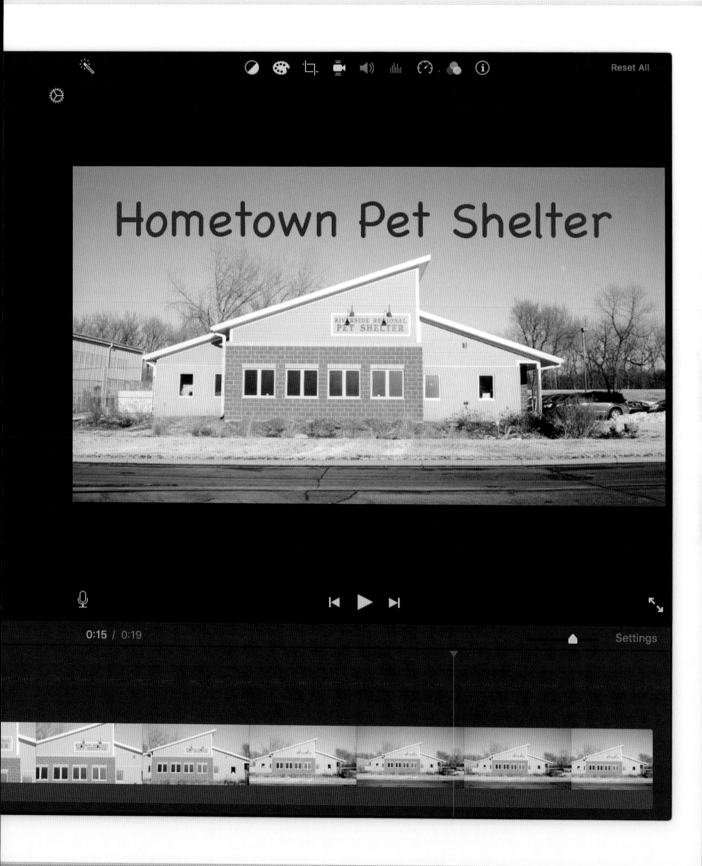

Documentary Debut

Sharing Your Video

Now that your video is all done, you'll want to share it with your soon-to-be fans. Make a big deal about it. You put a lot of hard work into this thing! Have a premiere night at your house, and invite your family to watch it. If your friends have made videos too, turn it into a film festival. Want to see whether people around the world will watch it? Ask your parents/guardians to help you upload it to the internet (YouTube, Vimeo).

That's a Wrap!

Now that you've created your first short documentary, go make another. Become an expert and explore a new topic. Using what you've learned, you can make something even better and more informative. With lots of practice, great things will happen. Your next short documentary will be nothing "short" of amazing!

PRO TIP

If you don't want to use your real name (or other identifying information), be sure to remove it from the video before posting it online!

Meet Your Film Instructor

Thomas Kingsley Troupe is an amateur filmmaker who has been making goofy movies and videos since he was in high school. Thomas has worked in the visual effects department for a handful of Hollywood movies and shows. He has also written and directed a number of short films for the 48 Hour Film Fest & Z Fest contests and loves creating funny videos with his own sons at home. Thomas says, "Making movies is the BEST. It can be a lot of work, but finishing a movie to show to your friends and family is WORTH IT!"

Read More

Asselin, Christine Carlson. *Smart Research Strategies: Finding the Right Sources.* Research Tool Kit. North Mankato, Minn.: Capstone Press, 2013.

Maura, Shauna. *Record It!: Shooting and Editing Digital Video.* Information Explorer Junior. Ann Arbor, Mich.: Cherry Lake Pub., 2013.

Internet Sites

Learn About Film: How to Make a Movie with Your iPhone or iPad
https://learnaboutfilm.com/iphoneipadfilm/filmmaking/

Glossary

app—a computer application

documentary—a movie about real events and people

edit—to cut and rearrange pieces of film to make a movie or TV program

narration—a speech delivered to accompany a movie, broadcast, etc.

rough cut—the first version of a movie after early editing

scene—a part of a story, play, or movie that shows what is happening in one place and time

scenic—creating a beautiful view

script—the story for a play, movie, or TV show

storyboard—a series of drawings that shows the plot of a TV show or movie

treatment—a detailed summary of a film

Apps and Software

iMovie, by Apple—an app to create your own movies

Movie Maker 10, by Microsoft—a full movie-making software for all budding artists

Imagemaker, by the Tiffen Company—changes a smartphone experience into a more traditional camera experience

Index